Watery Graves

CAROLE WILKINSON

HORWITZ
MARTIN

HORWITZ
MARTIN

Horwitz Martin Education
A Division of Horwitz
  Publications Pty Ltd
55 Chandos St
St Leonards NSW 2065
Australia

Horwitz Martin Education
Unit 15, Cressex Enterprise Centre
Lincoln Road
High Wycombe, Bucks HP12 3RL
United Kingdom

a black dog book
Designed by Josie Semmler
Illustrations by Peter Mather, pp. 3, 4, 5, 23, 25, 37, 38, 49, 50, 63, 65,
77, 79.
The publishers would like to thank the following for permission to
reproduce photographs and illustrations. Heritage Victoria, pp. 16,
33, 67, 72, 73, 83, 84, 89. Other images are from the editor's,
author's and designer's collections or are in the public domain.
Every effort has been made to contact original sources, where
known, for permissions. If an infringement has inadvertently
occurred, the editor wishes to apologise.
The publisher and the editor would like to thank Garry Chapman
and Vicki Hazell, the educational consultants on this series.

National Library of Australia
Cataloguing information
Wilkinson, Carole. 1950–
  Watery graves.

  ISBN 0 7253 1658 6.

  1. Shipwrecks - Juvenile literature.
  I. Title. (Series: Phenomena).

910.452

Printed and bound in Australia by
Sands Print Group Pty Ltd
2 3 4 5
00 01 02

Understanding the Horwitz Martin logo

Thoth
The Egyptian
god of wisdom,
mathematics and writing.

Contents

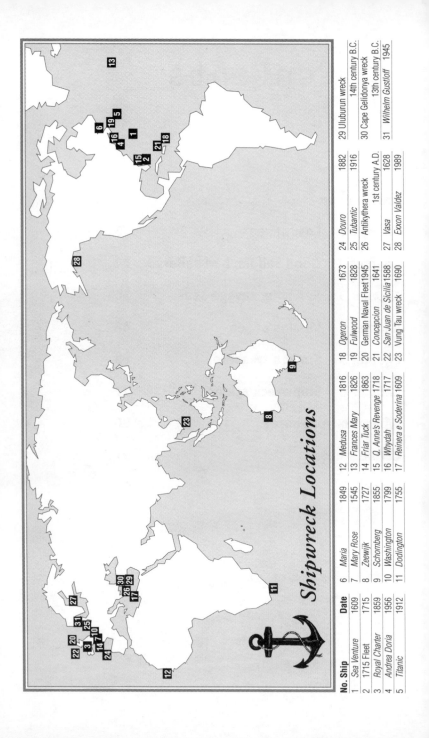

Shipwreck Locations

No.	Ship	Date
1	Sea Venture	1609
2	1715 Fleet	1715
3	Royal Charter	1859
4	Andrea Doria	1956
5	Titanic	1912

No.	Ship	Date
6	Maria	1849
7	Mary Rose	1545
8	Zeewijk	1727
9	Schomberg	1855
10	Washington	1799
11	Dodington	1755

No.	Ship	Date
12	Medusa	1816
13	Frances Mary	1826
14	Friar Tuck	1863
15	Q. Anne's Revenge	1718
16	Whydah	1717
17	Reinera e Soderina	1609

No.	Ship	Date
18	Ogeron	1673
19	Fulwood	1828
20	German Naval Fleet	1945
21	Concepcion	1641
22	San Juan de Sicilia	1588
23	Vung Tau wreck	1690

No.	Ship	Date
24	Douro	1882
25	Tubantic	1916
26	Antikythera wreck	1st century A.D.
27	Vasa	1628
28	Exxon Valdez	1989

No.	Ship	Date
29	Uluburun wreck	14th century B.C.
30	Cape Gelidonya wreck	13th century B.C.
31	Wilhelm Gustloff	1945

Introduction

Introduction

N O-ONE KNOWS EXACTLY
how many ships lie in
watery graves on the
bottom of the ocean, we can
only guess. People have
been building and sailing
boats for at least 11,000

years. Shipwreck experts estimate that
one tenth of all the ships ever built have
been wrecked. That means there must be
the remains of millions of ships lying on
the seabed.

When a ship is wrecked it is a tragedy.
The ship is damaged or destroyed, people
often die and goods are lost. Yet people
have always been fascinated by shipwreck
stories: tales of terrible storms, arrogant
captains and sunken treasure. Part of the
fascination of shipwreck stories is the
way people behave when facing the
prospect of a watery grave.

Sometimes all the skill in the world can't save a ship in a storm. At other times ships are wrecked in perfect weather because of bad sailors. Survival at sea can often have more to do with good luck than good sailing. The best sailors may end up on the bottom of the ocean when their luck turns bad, while good luck saves poor sailors in the worst situations.

The misfortune of unlucky sailors is sometimes transformed into good luck for the people who find the sunken ships. Treasure hunters might find gold coins, marine archaeologists might find a clue to the past through an ancient oil jar or the remains of a 16th-century sailor's shoe.

Every shipwreck has its own story. Sometimes it's the ship itself that is interesting, sometimes it's the way it sank that makes it special, other wrecks are interesting because of the way they are discovered. Each one has secrets to reveal about human nature.

For thousands of years ships have been sailing and sinking—taking passengers and crew with them. Yet we keep going out on the sea. Perhaps we think it won't be us. Do you feel lucky today?

chapter 1
Lost at sea

Imagine you are Amy Taylor sailing on the *Sea Venture* for the new colony of Virginia in 1609...

A MY WASN'T SUPPOSED to go on deck by herself, but the ship was rocking so much it made her feel sick to be down below. Her mother was asleep, surely she wouldn't mind if Amy went up on deck to her father?

They had been at sea for nearly two months and Amy was tired of being on the *Sea Venture*. She missed their little cottage and the green countryside that surrounded it. She missed the comforts of home: her own bed with the pink counterpane, the special cakes her mother made for her, her darling cat, Tom. She couldn't wait until they reached Virginia in seven or eight days time. She didn't know what to expect there. Did they have cats in Virginia? Whatever was in store for them, Amy was looking forward to setting foot on solid ground again.

A strong wind blew her hair into her eyes as she reached the top of the companionway. She had to hold onto the rail to make sure that a gust of wind didn't pick her up and carry her away as she searched the deck for her father.

The *Sea Venture* wasn't a big ship, so it didn't take long for Amy to find him standing on the bow with the Admiral, Sir George Somers. Amy was afraid of Sir George. Her father had assured her that he was friendly enough when you got to know him, but to Amy he seemed like a gruff old man who didn't like children. She decided to hide in a coil of rope until Sir George left and her father was by himself. The wind brought a fragment of their conversation to her.

"I have never before seen such dark and menacing clouds," Amy heard her father say.

"And the wind," said Sir George. "Have you ever heard such a sound?" The wind through the rigging sounded like wild animals, shrieking and wailing.

The two men started to move away together. Amy called out to her father, but the awful wind blew her words away and he kept on walking. The thick black clouds were now all around the ship. It seemed more like night than day. Rain started to pour down. The ship was pitching back and forth. Waves were washing over the bow. Amy was too scared to move. She clung onto the ropes with both hands and prayed for the storm to pass quickly.

It didn't pass quickly though. The storm just kept getting stronger and stronger. The rain became so heavy it seemed to Amy that a river of water was pouring from the sky. Amy was drenched. Sailors were climbing among the rigging, reefing the sails to slow the *Sea Venture*.

It seemed to make little difference; the wind still drove the ship on. It crashed into each wave with such force that Amy thought the ship would be broken to pieces. One moment the little ship was raised high up on an enormous mountain of water, the next it was sliding down the other side of the wave, so far down, Amy was sure they must be at the bottom of the ocean. She lost her grip on the ropes as a huge wave crashed over the bow.

Amy thought she would certainly be washed overboard, but a hand appeared out of the darkness and grabbed hold of her.

"This is no place for a child," the sailor shouted as he gathered her up and almost threw her down the nearest hatchway.

Below decks was a different sort of hell. The stench of vomit made her feel sick. The moans and cries of the passengers were awful to hear. Her mother grabbed Amy, who was shivering from cold and fear, and wrapped her in a blanket.

"I thought you were lost, my darling," she cried. "I wish we had never left England!"

The storm went on and on. The hatches were nailed shut to stop the water filling up the ship. Through the portholes there was nothing to see but inky black water and even blacker clouds. Amy lost track of time. The sky was so dark it was impossible to tell when day ended and night began. Amy thought that they would never see daylight again. She didn't wish for the comforts of home any more, all she wanted was for the sea to stop heaving, the ship to be still and to see blue sky again. ⚓ end

THE GIANT WAVES and ferocious winds Amy experienced really happened. The *Sea Venture* was one of nine ships carrying people to the new colony of Jamestown in Virginia. Sir George Somers was the admiral of the fleet. Everybody believed at the time that the *Sea Venture* and those on board had perished.

We'll find out what actually happened to the *Sea Venture* in Chapter 3, and whether the ship escaped a watery grave.

At the time of the wreck people were fascinated by the story of the *Sea Venture*. Several of those on board later wrote their stories, which became bestsellers. Amy's story is based on *The True Reportory of the Wracke* written by William Strachey, secretary to Sir George Gates, the newly appointed governor of the colony of Virginia. Amy is an imaginary character because little is known about the few children on the ship. We can only imagine how terrified they were.

"The cloudes gathering thicke upon us, and the windes singing and whistling most unusually, a dreadful storme and hideous began to blow."

From *The True Reportory of the Wracke* by William Strachey

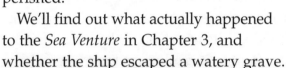

Inspiring or terrifying?

The terror of shipwrecks has always fascinated people. Strachey's dramatic account of the *Sea Venture* inspired William Shakespeare, the most famous playwright in the English language, to write his last play *The Tempest*. The play was performed in London only two years after the *Sea Venture* set sail.

The Tempest is a fantasy set on an island. The magician Prospero and his daughter Miranda are shipwrecked on an island. Prospero uses his magic to release good spirits imprisoned there by a witch.

Whether it is a luxury liner, a wooden treasure ship or a fishing boat, every shipwreck has a story to tell. Just as in Shakespeare's day, people are still fascinated by the devastating power of the wind and the ocean today. Look at how many books and films there are about the sinking of the *Titanic*.

The days of wood and sail

In the past, ships were made of wood and depended on the wind to fill their sails and carry them across the oceans. Sailing ships like the *Sea Venture* were often quite small. In those days, once a sailing ship left the shore, there was no way

At any given moment there are around 2000 storms raging at sea.

they could communicate with
people on land or with other ships
at sea. Those on board had only
themselves and their ship with
which to survive the sea. Sailors
were at the mercy of the elements.
They relied on their own skills to
forecast the weather and predict storms.
They also relied on sea charts to tell them
where dangerous rocks and reefs were.
Unfortunately the charts weren't always
accurate. Travelling by sea in the days of
wood and sail was a dangerous business.

> A superstition among sailors is that whistling can turn a gentle breeze into a dangerous storm.

Sailors' friend or foe?

Without wind, a sailing ship couldn't go
anywhere. So a good strong breeze was
just what sailors wanted. Once the wind
began to blow too strongly though, it
had the power to rip sails to shreds, to
break masts and even to capsize ships.
Sometimes a storm became a hurricane,
the worst sort of storm. Then the sailors'
friend, the wind, became a deadly enemy.

> capsize:
> *to overturn a boat accidentally.*

What are hurricanes?

The storm that almost sank the *Sea
Venture* was a hurricane. Hurricanes are

Hurricanes are ranked according to their strength. Category 1 hurricanes have winds of at least 120 kph and the strongest hurricanes, Category 5, have winds of more than 250 kph.

huge storms that blow-up near the equator. They are high-speed winds and can easily destroy ships. Hurricanes form in tropical oceans, where the air is humid and the sea is warm. As the air is warmed by the sea, it rises up to meet cooler air. The strong winds are caused by air rushing to replace the air that's rising. The result is a ferocious wind blowing in a circular motion.

Where are the worst winds?

The warm waters of the Gulf of Mexico, are a breeding ground for hurricanes. This is one of the most dangerous parts of the world for sailing ships. Spanish sailors around the 16th and 17th centuries discovered the dangers of sailing the Gulf as they headed north, ready to cross the Atlantic homeward bound for Spain.

Hurricanes still rage in the islands of the Carribean today.

Early in the 16th century, the Spanish had conquered much of South and Central America. The Spanish mined huge quantities of gold, silver and precious jewels in this New World. They then shipped their treasure home to Spain

through the Gulf of Mexico.

Once a year, a fleet of large Spanish ships, called galleons, left the Americas loaded with treasure, destined for the king in Madrid. Sailing in fleets guarded by armed ships was the best way for the Spanish to protect precious cargoes from pirates and the warships of rival European nations. Unfortunately, if a hurricane struck, the loss of treasure could be huge.

> Hurricanes are called cyclones by people in the South Pacific Ocean. The people of the North Pacific Ocean call them typhoons.

To avoid the hurricane season, the fleet had to set sail before June. Often there were delays. Sometimes, fleets didn't leave until July or August, the very worst time for hurricanes. During two hundred years of Spanish rule in the Americas, Spain lost hundreds of ships and tonnes of treasure to hurricanes—and also, as we will find out later, to pirates.

The shipwrecks of the Spanish Main, full of sunken treasure, have captured people's imagination. The chance of discovering treasure worth a fortune is one of the reasons why shipwrecks have continued to fascinate people for centuries.

> The Spanish Main is the Carribean Sea next to the Americas, between the isthmus of Panama and the mouth of the Orinoco.

The 1715 fleet

In the 16th century, cocoa was an exotic luxury for Europeans.

During 1715, treasure was piling up in warehouses at ports in the New World, waiting to be shipped to Madrid. No treasure ships had sailed to Spain for two years for fear of attack. The Spanish authorities decided they could wait no longer and loaded a fleet of twelve ships with treasure. Some of the treasure was a wedding present from the Spanish King Felipe V to his bride, Isabella.

The treasure that the Spanish ships carried wasn't only gold and jewels. It included cocoa and other goods that could not be found in Europe, such as vanilla, tobacco and tortoise shell. These days, a cup of cocoa isn't anything special, but in 1715 cocoa was a rare treat.

The fleet set sail from Havana on the island of Cuba on 27 July—after the hurricane season had already started. The ships sailed up the coast of Florida to catch the trade winds, which would help carry them across the Atlantic Ocean. After only four days at sea they ran into a hurricane and the ships were driven onto the reefs on the Florida coast, near what is

trade winds:
reliable winds which blow towards the equator.

today Cape Canaveral. Eleven ships sank. Only one survived. More than a thousand people drowned and the king's wedding presents sank to the bottom of the sea.

In Chapter 4, we'll see how these sunken ships inspired one man to become a pirate.

When the sea meets the shore

Winds can be terrifying, yet ships usually survive storms, even hurricanes, if they are out in the open sea. Ships have been carefully designed to make use of the wind and to withstand storms. A ship may lose its mast, its hull may be damaged, but the ship usually stays afloat. Ships are in most danger when they are in sight of land.

Most wrecks happen when the wind and waves drive ships onto rocks and reefs. With the ship pinned to the rocks, the sea can do its greatest damage. The force of the waves smashes the ship against rocks and wrecks it beyond saving. The smaller the boat, the less chance it has to survive. People sometimes escaped a sinking ship

reef:
1. to shorten the sail by rolling and tying, so there is less sail for the wind to blow against.
2. a narrow ridge of rocks, sand or coral at, or just below, the surface of the water.

in lifeboats and headed for the shore, only to be pounded against rocks by the waves.

How strong are waves?

A wave two metres high and a metre wide contains about four tonnes of water. That's about the weight of small truck. In severe storms, waves can be more forceful, breaking with a force of up to 32 tonnes per square metre. In a storm, a ship that is 100 metres long would have the equivalent weight of 200 semitrailers crashing into its side and ramming it against rocks.

No wonder waves can do so much damage.

Steampower versus wave power

You might think that once ships were built of iron and powered by steam they would be able to withstand storms. This wasn't always the case.

The *Royal Charter* was a big steam clipper made of iron which weighed 2719 tonnes. In 1859 it was sailing from Melbourne to Liverpool. Many of the passengers were returning from Australia after striking it rich in the

clipper:
a very fast sailing ship.

goldfields. They were nearly at their destination. Perhaps they were thinking that their luck had stayed with them, because the voyage of nearly 20,000 km had gone smoothly. Their luck was about to change though. The *Royal Charter* was caught in a fierce storm in the Irish Sea and driven onto the island of Anglesey. A huge wave crashed onto the ship and broke its iron hull in two.

The ship was smashed to pieces. Salvagers found a piece of iron from the ship with a gold bar and several gold coins embedded in it. The waves were so strong they had driven the gold into the iron as though it was as soft as cheese. Of the 388 passengers on board, only twenty survived. The rest were battered to death on the rocks by the waves.

Steam-driven paddle wheels were being fitted to boats as an alternative to sails in 1812. The screw propeller came into use in 1838.

Bound for India

Modern sailors have very accurate sea charts which tell them where every rock and reef is. When parts of the world were still unexplored, maps and sea charts were not always so reliable.

In 1755, a fleet of five British ships set

The sextant is an instrument that measures the position of the sun, moon or stars in the sky to help steer a ship's course.

sail for India. Aboard one of the ships was the statesman Robert Clive, known as Clive of India. He was famous for keeping control of India for Britain. His baggage, which included three chests of gold and silver, was stowed on a different ship—the *Dodington*. As the fleet sailed around the Cape of Good Hope at the bottom of Africa, the weather grew stormy and the *Dodington* lost sight of the other ships.

Chaos Island

The captain studied his charts and calculated the ship's course as best he could. His sextant was useless in the terrible weather. He headed north-east to make sure that they sailed further away from the dangerous, rocky coast.

Unfortunately, his charts were incorrect and the course he set aimed the ship straight at Chaos Island. The ship ran into the island and was completely wrecked in less than twenty minutes. More than 200 men, including the captain, lost their lives, and Clive of India never saw his chests of valuables again.

Chaos Island was in the wrong place on many 18th-century sea charts and the *Dodington* was not the first ship to be wrecked on it. British Navy charts at that time referred to it as Confused Island.

When mapmakers finally decided on its true location and positioned it correctly on charts, the island was not such a threat to safety at sea, and its name was changed to Bird Island.

Danger in still waters

Even when there is no wind, ships are still wrecked. Fog and ice are other weather conditions that can be dangerous. Colliding with other ships is a common cause of shipwreck.

The Italian liner *Andrea Doria* was one of the largest, fastest and most luxurious ships afloat in her day. In 1956 she was sailing from New York to Europe when she ran into thick fog off the US coast near Nantucket Island. (Windless conditions are perfect for fog to form.) In the same thick fog was the *Stockholm*, a Swedish ship.

The fog was so dense that radar

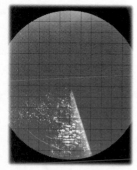

Radar equipment uses radio waves to detect the presence and location of an object.

was the only way one ship could tell where the other ship was. The crews misjudged their positions on the radar.

It wasn't until the ships suddenly saw each other's lights through the fog that both captains desperately turned their ships to avoid a collision. Unfortunately, they turned towards each other. The bow of the *Stockholm*, specially strengthened to break through ice, ripped a 10 metre gash in the starboard side of the *Andrea Doria*. Fifty-five passengers drowned.

An American coastguard vessel wanted to tow the damaged ship to shallow water, where she might have been saved, but the *Andrea Doria* was a foreign-owned ship and special permission had to be granted. Though the ship stayed afloat for twelve hours, it sank before the permit arrived.

Icebergs aren't so cool

starboard:
the right side of a ship or boat when facing the front or bow.

In colder parts of the world, sailors have to keep a sharp lookout for icebergs. Unlike reefs and rocks, icebergs can move and aren't marked on sea charts.

Another luxury liner, the *Titanic*, now perhaps the most famous shipwreck of all, was sailing from England to New York on its maiden voyage in 1912. The *Titanic* was famous as it was called the "unsinkable ship". Lookouts saw the iceberg in the darkness, but the ship was travelling too fast to avoid hitting it. Though the collision was hardly felt by the passengers, the ship sank in two hours.

An iceberg is a large mass of ice which has broken away from a glacier and floated out to sea.

There were not enough lifeboats on the ship for all the passengers and 1490 people died in the icy waters of the North Atlantic Ocean.

Another ship sunk by an iceberg was the *Maria*. She was on the last leg of a voyage from Ireland to Canada in 1849. The ship collided with an iceberg and sank with the loss of 109 lives. Three survivors were rescued from one of the ship's lifeboats and the following day nine more were found drifting on a chunk of ice.

Oily wreck

Nowadays sailors have modern navigational equipment and can communicate with the shore and other ships at all times. They have reliable charts and huge, strong ships made of steel. Even so ships still get wrecked.

A famous accident—and environmental disaster—of modern times is the *Exxon Valdez* incident. It was rocks, not ice, that brought this supertanker to a halt.

The *Exxon Valdez* is one of the largest vessels on water. Almost 300 metres long, it moves with tremendous force through the water. At its top speed of 25 kph, it would take 5 km for it to come to a halt.

On the 23 March, the ship set sail from Port Valdez in Alaska for Long Beach, California, five and half days away. As it was heading south through Prince William Sound, the ship changed course because some small icebergs (growlers) had drifted into the Sound from the Columbia Glacier. Growlers are chunks of ice that make a growling noise when knocked against the ship's hull.

Run aground

At four minutes past midnight on 24 March 1989, the *Exxon Valdez*, loaded with more than a million barrels of oil, ran aground on Bligh Reef.

It is not known whether the order to

change back to the original course was give too late, if the helmsman did not follow instructions properly, or if something was wrong with the steering system of the vessel.

The impact was so great that it ripped through the ship's cargo tanks, spilling tonnes of oil into the Sound so quickly that it created waves of oil a metre high. This was the worst oil spill in history. It killed 300,000 birds, 3500 otters and 200 harbour seals. The oil company owning the ship had to pay $5 billion for the damage caused.

Oil destroys the natural water-proofing of sea birds. Oil-drenched birds die of hunger or cold as they cannot go out to sea. Some birds are poisoned by the oil when they try to clean it from their feathers.

To the sea in ships

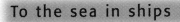

For centuries, ships have sailed the ocean transporting goods and people between countries and continents. The ocean is powerful and potentially dangerous. Even modern sailors know they need to treat the ocean with respect if they are to survive. Wind, storms, reefs, rocks and bad weather can quickly turn the sea into the sailor's enemy.

chapter 2
Good sailors, bad sailors

Imagine you are Dick Lacey, a young trumpeter on board one of Henry VIII's favourite ships, the *Mary Rose* in the year of 1545...

DICK STOOD on the deck of the *Mary Rose*, nervously polishing his trumpet on his sleeve. He had never felt so proud in his thirteen short years.

There was not a breath of wind in the air. For the past hour, the galleys from the French fleet had used their guns to pound the anchored English ships with round after round. The French galleys had oars, while the more manoeuvrable English ships depended on the wind. Without wind, the English ships couldn't move.

Then a light breeze blew up. A murmur of anticipation went up in the

English fleet as their ships swung towards the French. Whistles blew. Dick heard the chant of the sailors as they strained to haul up the heavy anchors of the fleet: "Haul! Haul! Haul one and all! Haul!" Dick's hands felt sweaty against the trumpet. He wiped them nervously on his tunic.

One of the officers called out Sir George Carew's order. Sir George was the captain of the *Mary Rose*, the king's favourite ship. The yardmen began to loose the sails.

"How are we supposed to fight with our bellies empty?" grumbled a sailor standing next to Dick.

"I couldn't eat if you paid me," said an archer. "My guts ache with sickness."

This was not how Dick had imagined sailors of the king would behave in his dreams of glory.

The sailors moved sluggishly into action. Dick watched as they threw a huge rope net over his head and across the main gundeck in the waist of the ship. Dick felt a little safer in this cage of ropes. The strong ropes of the net would stop any French soldiers boarding the ship. The soldiers and archers all took up position in the tall raised parts called castles at either end of the ship. There were more than 300 extra fighting men added to the *Mary Rose*'s usual crew.

"What does that puffed-up popinjay know about sailing a warship?" said one sailor softly. "I've served in more battles than he has."

"I think you should just obey your orders," Dick blurted out.

The sailor was about to clip Dick on the ear, when the ship heeled as the sails began to fill with wind. Dick took the opportunity to stagger out of the sailor's reach.

The officer was shouting more orders. The *Mary Rose* began to move off majestically towards the French fleet with her sails billowing, her flags and her pennants fluttering. Dick sighed with relief, at last they could attack the French.

The tilt on the deck steadily increased as the *Mary Rose* failed to settle back to an even keel. A shout came from below that the sea was pouring through the gunports. The guns and the cannonballs started to roll over to the side. The soldiers stumbled on the sloping decks. The boatswain frantically shouted orders to shorten sails. Sailors were scrambling to obey but were caught in the confusion of soldiers falling and tripping on the deck.

Cold green water was lapping onto the starboard decking. Cries of panic spread among the men. The boarding nets had them trapped like fish. Men were screaming as they slid down into the rising waters.

Dick began to slide also, but a hand behind him grasped his tunic at the neck. The sailor who had been ready to clip his ear had now saved him. The tilt on the deck was increasing. Dick watched frozen with fear as the water rose steadily higher up the deck each second. Men thrashed and struggled in the waters below. Dick knew that most, like him, couldn't swim. A body cannoned into him. He felt his tunic slide from the sailor's grip and Dick began to slip down towards the rising waters...

end

THE *MARY ROSE* turned over and sank in perfect weather killing most of the 700 men on board. Some of the men were later picked up by boats from the rigging, which poked above the waterline. We could speculate that perhaps the imaginary Dick Lacey was one of these. He might have found a hole in the boarding net large enough for a lad to wriggle through—and a safe spot on a mast to cling to.

So, why did the *Mary Rose* sink? It's one of the great historical mysteries. The French guns were yet to do damage. She had survived other battles and was one of the finest ships of the English fleet. Was it the poor discipline among the sailors? Were the men too sick or hungry to act quickly? Did the crew forget to close the gunports as the ship turned? Did the captain, Sir George Carew, who was also the vice-admiral of the fleet, order too tight a turn and the ship heeled too much, flooding the gunports?

Before refrigerators, sailors couldn't keep food fresh for long voyages. They had to eat food that lasted a long time, such as dried meat.

No-one really knows why the *Mary Rose* sank. Historians have developed theories about why the ship sank by sifting through records of previous battles and finding comments by people at the time. Most theories blame the sailors in some way, either the captain or the crew—or both.

Sir George Carew, on the *Mary Rose*, is supposed to have yelled to a kinsman on a passing ship that the sailors on board were "the sort of knaves I cannot rule".

The top job at sea

Ships' captains are responsible for the safety of the ship, its cargo and passengers. Captains make many decisions. They must carefully choose a safe course, so that the ship doesn't run into islands, reefs, lighthouses or other ships. They must decide how to handle the ship in storms. They must make sure that the ship is kept in good seaworthy condition, tell the crew what to do and keep good discipline. Often they were responsible for raising their own crews—and they were responsible for keeping their crews well-fed and healthy.

Not all captains do their job well. Sometimes

A skilled captain could maintain a disciplined crew who worked as a team. A bad captain with an unhappy crew could end up with a mutiny on his hands.

sailors refuse to obey their captain.
Sometimes good captains make mistakes.
Sometimes skillful sailors and captains do
their best, but luck is against them.

Crime and punishment

Jan Steyns was a skillful sailor. He was
the captain of a Dutch ship called the
Zeewijk carrying supplies across the
Indian Ocean to the Dutch colony in
Batavia in 1727. Also on board were three
tonnes of gold and silver.

The Dutch were aware of Australia's
existence long before the island was
claimed by the British. On their way to
Batavia, Dutch ships sometimes caught
sight of the western shore of the
land which they called *Terra Australis
Incognita* which means "the Unknown
Southland".

Captain Steyns worked for a shipping
company called the Dutch East India
Company which had strict regulations for
ships' captains. They were supposed to
sail along the known routes and
stay well clear of the coast of the
great Southland. Captain Steyns
didn't follow the rules. He

The city of Batavia
is known today as
Jakarta and is the
capital of Indonesia.

changed his course, looking for a better route, and sailed the *Zeewijk* straight into the Houtman Abrolhos reefs.

The ship was wrecked and only 88 of the 208 crew managed to struggle ashore onto a small island just four miles long. The ship's long boat was saved and ten men set sail for help. They were never seen again.

Captain Steyns tried to fix his mistake. He ordered the survivors to build another boat using wood from their wrecked ship. It took ten months of exhausting labour to complete this task. Finally, the captain stowed the boxes of gold and silver into the boat and the survivors set sail.

Fair punishment?

This time they were lucky and the makeshift boat arrived safely in Batavia. Even though Captain Steyns had survived a terrible ordeal and delivered the treasure safely, the Dutch East India Company punished him. He was charged and found responsible for the shipwreck. His punishment after months of hardship seems extremely harsh. He was tied to a

Sailors were proud of the figurehead on their ship and somewhat super-stitious about it. They kept it in good repair and relied on it to lead their ship safely and swiftly over the seas.

pole and beaten with rods. Then he was forced to labour in chains and without wages for fifteen years. That's not all, he also had to pay for the court costs!

Not all captains were treated so harshly. Some have been very neglectful and gotten away with it.

Speed kills

In the last century the only way to get from Europe to Australia was by sailing ship. The journey took about 120 days. Passenger and merchant ships wanted to get there and back again as quickly as possible. Because the ships couldn't travel any faster, the only thing sailors could do was to find a shorter route.

Navigators calculated that the shortest route to Australia from Europe is south across the middle of Antarctica and then north up to Australia. This route is impossible.

If ships could skirt around Antarctica as close as they could get, they could still cut many kilometres (and days) off their journey. On the return journey the ship would follow the currents around the other side of

The maximum speed of a sailing ship was 28 kph.

Antarctica, sailing past the tip of South America. This new route became known as the Great Circle Route.

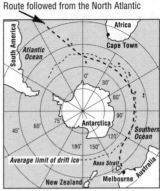
Route followed from the North Atlantic

The shorter route was more dangerous. Sailing so close to Antarctica, they had to battle furious gales, ride huge seas and dodge icebergs. Some captains took their ships too close. They arrived in Australia with torn sails and missing masts. Others disappeared without a trace.

"Bully" Forbes

The British clipper ship the *Schomberg*, was expected to break the record for the fastest voyage from Europe to Australia. It was a fine ship with the best and the biggest of everything. It had velvet pile carpets and furniture upholstered with gold satin. One sofa was big enough to seat 30 people.

Captain James "Bully" Forbes was in command of the *Schomberg* on her very first voyage. He got his nickname because of his reckless sailing techniques, his bad temper and his obsession with speed.

On an earlier voyage, he suspected that his crew might desert him and head for the goldfields. He pretended they had committed crimes and had them arrested. They stayed in jail until he was ready to sail. Another time he told the authorities there was disease on board and had the ship quarantined so that the crew couldn't leave.

A world record of 63 days for the trip from England to Australia by a sailing ship was set in 1854 and has never been broken.

He was so determined to break the record that he flew signal flags that said "Melbourne in 60 Days". Bad weather put a stop to Forbes's plans. Bully Forbes was angry that he'd missed a chance to beat the record. He lost interest in the voyage and was playing cards below decks when the first mate reported that the ship was getting too close to the shore.

He finished his card game before he went on deck to order a change of course. By then it was too late, the *Schomberg* ran onto a reef. Forbes was more annoyed at the inconvenience than worried about the danger to his passengers. He went back below decks trusting that the wind would blow the ship off the reef.

Luckily for the passengers, a steamer

came to their rescue. The first mate organised their transfer to safety. The *Schomberg* was dashed to pieces on the reef. Passengers complained that Captain Forbes was to blame for the loss of the *Schomberg*. He was found not guilty—though he was never again asked to command another great ship.

The Schomberg Chalice: a wine cup found in the watery grave of the *Schomberg*.

Scurvy dogs

"Bully" Forbes was a bad sailor because he was proud and careless. Some sailors during the great age of sail were poor sailors because they were sick. When sailors were at sea for months at a time their diet was poor. They had to live on preserved foods such as salted meat and hardtack. If they were lucky they might have a few hens on board to provide eggs. Because they rarely ate fresh fruit and vegetables they didn't get enough vitamin C, and that causes a disease called scurvy.

Sailors with scurvy got inflamed gums and horrible sores on their bodies. Their teeth fell out and they felt extremely tired and dejected. They imagined that they saw terrible things.

steamer: *a ship powered by steam.*

hardtack: *a hard, long-lasting biscuit.*

33

Sailors who fell ill with scurvy usually died. Sometimes half a ship's crew would be dead or dying from scurvy. Then doctors discovered that lack of vitamin C was the cause. From about 1795, sailors drank lime juice daily to combat scurvy.

A burning problem

In the days of wooden ships, fire was one of the greatest threats as there was plenty to burn. As well as the wood of the ship's hull and decks, there was the rigging and acres of canvas, sometimes barrels of gunpowder and flammable cargo like cotton. Fires could be easily started as all the lights were oil lamps or candles and all the cooking was done over open fires. Sailors weren't always as careful as they should have been. If a ship did catch fire it was still hard to put out the fire, even though it was surrounded by water, due to the ineffective hand-operated pumps.

flammable:
anything which catches fire easily.

Fire below

The *Washington* was anchored off Plymouth in 1799 with its holds full of bales of cotton from America. One of the crew spotted a British Navy press gang coming to force them into the service of the Navy. This was something that sailors always feared. The whole crew rushed to hide. The ship's cook dropped his knife as he was hurrying through the hold. He struck a light so that he could find the knife and accidentally set fire to a bale of cotton. The fire quickly spread through the cargo. The ship burned for nearly 24 hours and was totally destroyed.

Risky business

Bad weather can destroy a ship but bad sailors can be just as deadly. Sailors may make mistakes but captains have the ultimate responsibility for their ship. If they don't do their job well, then passengers and cargo are at great risk. If you are sailing on a ship, you should choose your captain carefully—and hope he has a good crew!

press gang:
a group of men with a commanding officer, who travelled around forcing other men into service in the army or navy.

chapter 3
Surviving savage seas

Imagine you have found the diary of Monsieur Savigny. The year is 1816...

OUR PLIGHT is unimaginable. We have been on this wretched raft for four days, and what a terrible state we are in. I can hardly believe it, but there are only fifteen of us left from the 150 who started on the raft. These few logs bound together with rope hardly deserve to be called a raft. When we were first cut loose it was so crowded our combined weight sank the raft so that we were standing waist-deep in water. Even now, though there are so few of us left, our weight still pushes the raft underwater.

At first, the weather was against us. Two nights of dreadful storms drowned many and washed away what food and water we had. Only wine and a few biscuits remain. The sun shines mercilessly by day and burns our skin.

On the third night, the soldiers drank too much wine. I have seen cases of delirium before, but never seen it strike so fast and so completely. They thought that we were enemies and attacked us with knives and swords. If they lost their weapons then they savaged us with their bare hands and teeth. They were like mad men. I had to fight for my life against men who were once my friends.

The first light showed the raft was covered with dead bodies. We threw the bodies into the sea. Then we made a terrible decision. The wounded were also thrown overboard, so that our meagre supplies are not wasted on the dying. That is not the worst of it.

Later we pulled some of the dead bodies out of the sea. These we are going to eat. At first, I was horrified, then after another day of starvation and thirst, I ate some of the human flesh.

We are a pitiful sight. Crazed and hungry, our bodies are covered in sores from wounds, from sunburn and from

being constantly covered with seawater.
Some were so desperate that they threw
themselves into the sea among the sharks
that constantly circle us. The remaining
soldiers may turn mad again and attack
us at any moment. Even one of my
friends might imagine I am an enemy and
fall on me with his sword.

The strangest thing happened. Our
miserable raft was suddenly surrounded
by a swarm of white butterflies. Though
some tried to grab them and eat them,
they were a sign of hope. I found the
courage to carry on. I managed to
convince everybody to throw all their
weapons in the sea.

At least now, if we all die on this
dreadful raft, it will not be at the hands of
each other. We have given up all hope of
reaching land and pulled down the sail.
We have used it to make a tent so that at
least we are protected from the sun. I will
lie back and give myself up to the visions
of green fields that fill my head.

end

THE FRIGATE *Medusa* was on its way to the French colony of Senegal in 1816 with 240 passengers and 160 crew members on board. Among the passengers were the new governor of Senegal and his family. The ship was sailing down the coast of Africa in an area known for uncharted sandbanks.

The captain, a man named de Chaumareys, was celebrating the ship crossing the Tropic of Cancer. He left the *Medusa* in the hands of one of the passengers. The amateur navigator miscalculated and drove the ship straight onto the Arguin Bank.

There were only six lifeboats on board the *Medusa*, not enough to take all the passengers and crew. De Chaumareys jumped out of a porthole to make sure he was in one of the boats. His officers, the governor and his family filled the boats. The remaining crew, soldiers and passengers, 149 people altogether, had to make do with a hastily built raft.

The boats were supposed to tow the raft but, before they had got far, the sailors in the boats let go of the ropes. The people on the raft were left to fend for themselves.

"They attacked us: we charged them in our turn, and immediately the raft was strewn with bodies. Those of our adversaries who had no weapons, endeavoured to tear us with their sharp teeth."

From the account of the raft of the *Medusa* by Henri Savigny and Alexandre Corréard.

frigate:
small warship often used for special missions.

A French painter named Géricault was so affected by the awful story of the *Medusa* that he painted a huge canvas of the raft and its miserable survivors. He shaved his head and shut himself in his studio and only came out when the painting was finished.

After 16 days of torture, a ship found them. The ship had not been sent to look for survivors, but to save the 90,000 francs which had been left on board the *Medusa*.

Once the survivors were returned to safety, Henri Savigny and Alexandre Corréard wrote about their ordeal. Their account shocked the people of France and Captain de Chaumareys was charged. The story you just read is based on this account.

One of the fascinations of shipwrecks is discovering who escaped a watery grave—and how they survived. It is said that on the shoulders of drowning fishermen you can sometimes see the boot marks of others more desperate to live.

Captain's crime

The idea of the captain being the last to leave a sinking ship is not just a noble gesture. It is naval law. Disobeying it is a serious crime and at the time of the *Medusa* it was punishable by death.

Captain de Chaumareys was struck off the navy list. He was not sentenced to death though. Instead, he was imprisoned for five years. Do you think his punishment fair in comparison to that of Captain Steyns, who even had to pay his own court costs?

Géricault's famous painting of the raft of the *Medusa* has served as a model for other artworks showing the desperation to survive after a shipwreck.

What's for dinner?

Another gruesome story of castaways comes from the survivors of the *Frances Mary*.

In 1826, Miss Ann Saunders was sailing home to England from America. She was travelling as female companion to Mrs Kendall, who was the wife of the ship's captain. Also on board was Miss Saunders's fiancé, James Frier. He was paying for his passage on the ship by working as a cook.

During the first couple of weeks of the voyage, they enjoyed pleasant weather. On 1 February, they ran into a storm that lasted for two days and badly damaged the ship. Then, when they thought the worst was over, an enormous wave crushed the stern.

stern: *the back part of a ship.*

Although water filled the ship the cargo of timber made the ship almost impossible to sink. The crew quickly scrambled to rescue the food supplies. They only managed to salvage some bread and cheese though.

A tent was made on the deck for shelter. The captain was forced to reduce rations to a quarter of hardtack biscuit per day. With no masts or sails the ship drifted helplessly at the mercy of the sea. Two ships were sighted, but neither came to help. By 11 February, they had no food left. Exhausted, sailors started to die of starvation.

The flesh of the dead

Cannibalism is the practice of eating your own species.

The following day, someone suggested that the only way that they would survive was by eating the flesh of the dead. Miss Saunders refused to eat the human flesh for 24 hours, but hunger forced her to give in. The next day they cut the heart and liver from a dead crewman and ate them. Seven others died almost immediately, including James Frier. Miss Saunders fought for her right to her fiancé's body.

While the rest of the crew were too weak to move. Miss Saunders found the strength to cut up and clean the flesh from the dead bodies. Her gruesome dedication kept them all alive.

Finally, on 7 March, after drifting for more than a month, a ship rescued them. Miss Saunders recovered from her ordeal and wrote an article titled *Narrative of the Shipwreck and Suffering of Miss Ann Saunders*.

The abandoned *Frances Mary* drifted at sea for several months before an English ship salvaged it. It was towed to Jamaica and made seaworthy again.

Paradise Island

Not all stories of castaways are as blood-curdling as the story of the *Mary Frances*. Do you remember the poor people in the *Sea Venture* in Chapter 1? We left them in the midst of a terrible storm which went on for four whole days. The ship was leaking so badly, the captain knew they were about to sink. He desperately scanned the horizon and to his delight he saw a speck of land. He sailed the sinking

One survivor of the *Sea Venture*, John Rolfe, later married the Indian Princess Pocahontas. Their story is the basis for the Disney animated film.

ship straight towards the island and rammed the crippled ship on shore as the sea was about to swamp it.

Miraculously, no-one was hurt and the passengers all cheered their captain. The Captain's smile soon faded when he realised that they were wrecked on Devil's Island. A small piece of land feared and avoided by all sailors.

Devil's Island?

They soon realised that there were neither devils nor people living on the island. To their surprise, they discovered it was a paradise. Today this island is called Bermuda.

There was plenty of fruit, wild pigs, birds and seafood to live on, as well as cedar forests to build with. The *Sea Venture* survivors lived very comfortably on the island for 42 weeks. During that time, they built two new boats.

Ten months after they were thought to be lost at sea, the *Sea Venture* survivors arrived in Virginia. The survivors were in much better shape than the

Survivors of a Dutch ship, wrecked off China in 1654, were held captive on an island and used as slaves for 13 years before they were able to steal a boat and escape to Japan.

colonists in Virginia who had little food, were suffering from disease and were afraid of attack by Indians.

Real-life Robinson Crusoe

One of the most famous shipwreck stories, *Robinson Crusoe*, is based on a true story. In 1719, the author, Daniel Defoe, was inspired by the story of a man who chose to be marooned on an island.

A Scottish man named Alexander Selkirk was sailing with Captain William Dampier in 1708. Dampier, though a good explorer and navigator, was a poor captain who often quarrelled with his men. After a dream that the ship would be wrecked, Selkirk decided he would be better off marooned on one of the Juan Fernandez islands.

The island he chose is a dot in the Pacific Ocean 800 kilometres from the coast of Chile. Selkirk had been to the island before and knew it had a good climate and that there was plenty of water and wild goats. So he was left ashore with just a few clothes, some blankets, a gun, a hatchet, a knife, a kettle and a Bible.

maroon: *to leave someone stranded on an island on purpose.*

"The Rats gnaw'd his Feet and Clothes while asleep, which oblig'd him to cherish the Cats with his Goats'-Flesh; by which many of them became so tame that they would lie about him in hundreds and soon deliver'd him from the Rats."

From the journal of Captain Woodes Rogers, on finding Selkirk.

For a while he regretted his rash decision. Rats gnawed at his feet at night, and by day he was lonely and miserable. As time passed, he began to get used to his solitary life. He tamed goats and wild cats to keep him company. He built two huts and amused himself by singing psalms and dancing with the cats. There was plenty of food to eat: goat meat, wild turnips, fish and turtle, all flavoured with pimento, a wild spice.

Selkirk felt his life was one long feast. When his clothes wore out, he made clothing from goatskin. He became so fit that he could outrun the goats.

When Dampier passed the island again four years and four months later, he saw smoke from a fire. He found Selkirk on shore looking as wild as his goats. Selkirk wasn't sure he wanted to return to civilisation, but he did in the end decide to return. In later years he became wealthy, but claimed, "I will never be so happy as when I was not worth a farthing."

psalms: *sacred or holy songs.*

Feathered survivors

Not all shipwreck survivors are human. The clipper *Friar Tuck* was returning to

England with a cargo of China's best tea in 1863. During a severe storm, the ship sheltered in a harbour on Taylor's Island, one of the Scilly Isles. The winds were too strong, though, and the ship was driven onto rocks. The residents of the island managed to salvage and hide most of the tea before the coastguards arrived. As well as the tea, they found some Chinese geese on board. Descendants of these geese still live in the grounds of Tresco Abbey on one of the Scilly Isles.

> Around half the ships that sailed in the 18th and 19th centuries were wrecked—that's about 600,000 shipwrecks.

Strange tales

Shipwreck survivors have many strange tales to tell. Being a castaway brings out the best qualities in some people, in others it brings out the worst. How do you think you would cope if you were cast adrift at sea?

chapter 4
Villains at sea

Imagine you are Israel Hands, first mate aboard the pirate ship *Queen Anne's Revenge* in 1718...

T HE WIND WAS BLOWING hard, and sharp needles of rain beat against Israel's face. But he'd been at the wheel of the *Queen Anne's Revenge* in worse storms.

Six months ago, the ship had had a different name and a different captain. Now she was the flagship of the dreaded pirate Edward Teach, more often called Blackbeard by those who feared him. Below decks was a cargo of gold, silver and jewels taken from the 18 ships that they had captured since stealing the *Queen Anne's Revenge* from the French. Soon Teach would be dividing up the booty. Israel was dreaming of what it would be like to be a rich man.

Suddenly Israel was being roughly pushed aside by his captain. "I'll take the wheel," shouted Teach. "You can't handle the ship in a storm, you fool."

Israel reluctantly gave up the wheel. He feared Teach's uncertain temper. Once, when drinking, Teach had suddenly drawn his pistols and fired under the table, wounding Israel in the knee. Israel still limped because of the bullet lodged in his knee. Teach had boasted that if he didn't kill one of his men now and then they'd forget who he was.

The ship lurched suddenly and Israel was thrown to the deck.

"Confound this foul weather," shouted Teach. "We've run aground."

The pirate ran the length of the deck shouting, his blood-red coat flapping, his swords and pistols clanking at his sides. "All hands below to man the pumps before we sink!"

Israel struggled to his feet and looked over the side. The bow of the ship was firmly buried in a sandbank. There seemed to be little damage. Why was Teach acting as if they were about to sink? Most of the pirate crew scurried fearfully below to obey their captain.

Israel stayed where he was.

Blackbeard was a huge man, but he could move quickly when he wanted to. Before Israel could form a plan to stop him, Teach and six of his closest henchmen had lowered a longboat and jumped into it.

Israel made a move to follow them. Teach drew one of his pistols and fired. The bullet hit the mast behind Israel's head. Blackbeard wasn't trying to frighten Israel, he was aiming to kill.

The pirates rowed for all they were worth and in a few minutes they had reached one of Teach's other ships. As Israel peered through a telescope, he saw the ship set sail leaving the *Queen Anne's Revenge* stuck on the sandbank.

A horrible thought struck Israel and he rushed below. Sure enough, the holds which the day before had been packed with gold and treasure, were now empty.

Israel ran back on deck in a fury, his dreams of wealth ruined. "I hope you die a horrible death," screamed Israel across the sea. "I hope it happens soon."

end

THE PIRATE BLACKBEARD got his name because of the thick black beard that covered almost his whole face. He was a big man who dressed in a red coat and carried lots of

> Captain Hook, in J.M. Barrie's story *Peter Pan*, is believed to be inspired by the real-life pirate Blackbeard.

weapons. He aimed to frighten his victims just by looking at them. To add to his terrifying appearance he tied slow fuses in his beard. He lit them whenever he was capturing a ship. When his victims saw the huge pirate with sparks and smoke coming off him, they usually surrendered without a fight.

Teach's downfall

Israel Hands got his wish. Blackbeard died a few months later in November 1718. He was killed during a fight with Lieutenant Robert Maynard, a British naval officer. Legend has it that it took five musket-ball wounds and twenty sword wounds to kill the pirate. Maynard claimed a reward of £100 and hung the pirate's head from the bowsprit. Israel and the other pirates were eventually captured and found guilty of piracy. The remains

> **bowsprit:**
> *a pole sticking out of the bow of a ship to which a sail is attached.*

of a ship believed to be the *Queen Anne's Revenge* were found in 1996. The records of the pirates' trial provided important clues that helped to locate the wreck.

Piracy

In the days of sailing ships it was considered bad luck to be able to swim.

The 16th and 17th centuries were the golden age of piracy. With shiploads of treasure sailing the seas, piracy was very tempting. Pirates were particularly common around the Caribbean where the Spanish treasure ships could be found. There were plenty of lonely islands in this part of the world where pirates could make their headquarters. The islands were full of deserted, shipwrecked and abandoned sailors, so crews for pirate ships were easily found.

Pirates didn't usually wreck ships on purpose like Blackbeard did. They tried to capture ships either to use themselves or to sell. Pirates weren't always the best sailors, though, and sometimes they sank their own ships!

Robin Hood of the seas

When Samuel Bellamy heard about the wreck of the 1715 fleet of Spanish treasure ships (we read about these in Chapter 1) he decided to try his hand at treasure hunting. When he reached the Caribbean though, he found that others had beaten him to it. Bellamy liked the idea of making a living by finding treasure. Why wait around for treasure ships to sink? Wouldn't it be much easier to capture ships before they sank? He decided to become a pirate.

> In the early 1600s, an estimated 500 pirate ships were terrorising the Mediterranean.

The *Whydah*

One of Bellamy's greatest prizes was a three-masted English galley called the *Whydah,* which he captured in 1717. The *Whydah* was a slave ship that had delivered its "cargo" of slaves to Jamaica and was on its way back to England with its holds full of sugar, indigo, gold and silver. The pirate and his crew chased the *Whydah* for three days before her captain eventually surrendered.

No-one was killed in the capturing of the *Whydah*. Bellamy wasn't a murderous rogue. In fact, he saw himself as a Robin Hood of the seas, robbing the rich to give to the poor (himself and his

> **galley:** *a fighting ship using oars and sails.*

In 1696, Captain Kidd was commissioned by the King of England to capture pirates. Instead, he became a pirate himself—but not for long. Kidd was tried and hanged at Execution Dock in 1701.

crew). He often urged the captive ship's crew to turn pirate and help him steal from the selfish rich people of the world. "They rob the poor under the cover of law," he once said. "We plunder the rich under protection of our own courage." If the crew refused to join him he called them "snivelling puppies" and "a parcel of hen-hearted numbskulls".

The Robin Hood of the seas wasn't around for long. After capturing a ship with a cargo of wine on its way to New York, Bellamy and his crew celebrated by drinking their loot. They ran into a storm and couldn't handle the ship in their drunken state. The ship struck a bank near Cape Cod and the *Whydah* became Bellamy's watery grave.

Sam Bellamy's career as a pirate lasted for just over a year, but in that time he captured more than 50 ships.

A sinking feeling

John Ward was short, bald and 50 years old when he became a pirate in 1603—not the typical image of a pirate in story-books. He roamed the Mediterranean capturing merchant ships. One ship that

Ward captured was a Venetian trading ship called *Reinera e Soderina*. Ward boldly sailed his ship alongside the *Reinera*. He arranged all of his men on deck each with a weapon so that it looked like he had a huge army. Instead of firing warning shots, they fired straight at the crew, hitting two of them. The crew of the *Reinera* were terrified and they offered no resistance when the pirates came aboard.

The *Reinera e Soderina* wasn't built to be a warship. Her planks began to rot under the weight of the guns. She began to leak badly and sank in 1609 near the Greek island of Kythera. Ward had moved to another ship by this time, but the crew of 400 drowned.

The plague of the sea

A pirate's career is usually short and most die young. John Ward was different. He retired from pirating and went to live in Tunis. He built a palace made of alabaster and marble and became a Muslim. In his old age Ward amused himself by experimenting with hatching chicken's eggs in camel dung. He died in his 70s of the plague.

Caribbean catastrophe

One of the pirate headquarters in the Caribbean was the tiny French island of Tortuga, near Haiti. The governor, Monsieur Bertram Ogeron, sent a specially built warship (which he named the *Ogeron* after himself) to capture the Dutch island of Curaçao. The ship's crew were pirates. They didn't get far. The *Ogeron* was wrecked on rocks near Puerto Rico. One account says the ship "broke into a thousand pieces". The crew travelled overland to Puerto Rico, but they were discovered by local Spaniards who apparently cried, "Ha! Ye thievish dogs, here's no quarter for you," and massacred the defenceless pirates.

Bungling buccaneers

The schooner *Fulwood* was sailing to England from Canada in 1828 with a cargo of wooden chests. The crew knew exactly what was in the chests. They were filled with Spanish doubloons that were being sent to England as payment for goods. They had barely got clear of the Canadian coast when the crew killed the captain and the ship's officers and seized the gold. Unfortunately, they hadn't left anyone alive who knew how to navigate. The ship was wrecked before they were out of Canadian waters. The pirates managed to save the chests of gold and bury them on an island, but they were captured and hanged before they could enjoy their ill-gotten gains.

Wreckers

You might think that the rule of "finders keepers" applies to shipwrecks. Yet even when wrecked on a foreign shore, a ship and its cargo still belong to its owners.

Last century, shipwrecks were a more common event. Local residents often rescued and took care of survivors. It was also their job to bury the dead. Most of them believed they had a right to salvage whatever they could before any officials arrived, regardless of the law.

"Finders keepers" was the common, if illegal, practice for those who buried the bodies from shipwrecks.

Wreckers were not looking for treasure. They were happy to find crates of everyday items such as crockery, clothing or blankets that they could use or sell. Alcohol was a popular find. Everything which could be used was stripped from the wreck. Timber was salvaged for building or for firewood and other items such as chains and copper were also claimed.

Some wreckers didn't wait for the sea to provide them with wreckage. They lured ships onto rocks by covering lighthouse lights and lighting fires on hilltops. If survivors made it back to shore they could be murdered and their bodies robbed.

Do pirates still roam the seas?

Though there are no longer shiploads of renegades flying the Jolly Roger, piracy does still exist. Modern acts of piracy range from thieves in speedboats boarding ships and ferries and robbing passengers, to heavily armed gangs taking over huge tankers. Nowadays, pirates are looking for cargoes of modern "treasure" such as electronic goods and oil. Modern pirates, like those from earlier days, will take anything of value. Cargoes as diverse as sugar and

Jolly Roger:

one of several different flags flown on pirate ships. The Jolly Roger is a black flag with a white skull and crossed thigh bones on it.

typewriters have been hijacked in recent years. Even today, captured ships are far too valuable to sink. Instead of adding a ship to their armada, pirates rename the vessel and sell it to an unsuspecting buyer.

In 1997, 229 incidents of piracy were reported around the world.

Heroes or villains?

Bad weather or bad sailing are not the only reasons why ships sink. What's more, people who sink ships on purpose may not always be thought of as villains. The purpose of a warship is to deliberately sink other ships. In war each side thinks they are heroes and their enemies are villains.

The first warships only had battering rams, archers and men with spears. Later, huge catapults were fitted on board. These weapons were most deadly when a burning ball of Greek Fire (a mixture of pitch, oil, charcoal, sulphur, phosphorus and salt) was hurled at enemy ships.

Guns were first mounted onto ships five centuries ago. At first, ships were too unstable to cope with heavy, powerful guns so most

When the German ocean liner *Wilhelm Gustloff* was hit by a Russian torpedo during World War II, over 7000 refugees and wounded soldiers died.

battles were fought at close range with smaller guns. The guns were mounted on the sides of the ships so that to shoot at each other ships had to be sailing alongside each other. It wasn't until 1854 that the gun turret was developed allowing guns to face any direction.

Scuppered

You would expect navy commanders to always sink enemy ships, but occasionally they sink their own. At the end of the First World War, when Germany surrendered to the Allied powers, the German forces were disarmed. The German Navy had to sail all its ships to a natural deepwater harbour in the remote Orkney Islands north of Scotland. The British Navy kept watch over the crew of the 74 German boats.

scupper:

to sink your ship on purpose.

semaphore:

to convey information using signals (often flags).

Rear Admiral Reuter didn't like the idea of his ships being handed over to the British.

One afternoon, when the British ships were all out on

manoeuvres, he quietly spread his orders by semaphore. The entire fleet was to be scuppered by opening the seacocks. A group of children on a school excursion watched in amazement as all the ships hoisted the German flag and then started to sink together.

The only sound was of the air escaping from below decks and bubbling to the surface as some of the finest warships of the day sank.

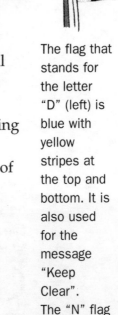

The flag that stands for the letter "D" (left) is blue with yellow stripes at the top and bottom. It is also used for the message "Keep Clear". The "N" flag is blue and white check. It also means "Negative" or "No".

chapter 5
Sunken treasure

Imagine you are Francis Rogers, the captain of one of three ships searching for sunken Spanish treasure. The year is 1686...

"COME IN and sit down Francis," William Phips said as he invited Francis Rogers into his cabin. Francis glanced nervously around the cramped cabin. The narrow bed was littered with sea charts and astronomical tables for calculating the ship's position.

Francis sat down at the small table, which was already set for dinner. A cabin boy came in and served smoked ham and boiled potatoes. The ale in their pewter tankards rocked gently with the motion of the ship. Mr Phips didn't say a word as they ate the food.

62

"Why has he invited me?" thought Francis. He touched the cold metal object under his coat. "He doesn't know my secret. He can't."

It wasn't until the cabin boy had taken away the dirty plates and lit the candles that Mr Phips started to talk.

"Francis, I don't have to tell you that it has been my dream, some might say my obsession, to find the *Concepcion* and all the Spanish silver that she holds."

"Of course not, sir," said Francis.

"It is six years since I first learned about the *Concepcion*."

"I have heard the story. An old sailor, the only survivor of the wreck, told you that she went down on this reef near a pinnacle of rock."

"I know some of the crew think I am foolish to base my dream on such flimsy evidence."

Francis wiped a spot of gravy from the lace cuff of his shirt and didn't say anything. He had overheard such comments.

"I have tried my hardest, Francis," went on Mr Phips, draining his tankard.

"I have dedicated myself to the task of finding the *Concepcion*."

"You have done everything a man could do."

"Yes, for a simple ship's carpenter who could not read and write, I think I have achieved something."

"You have indeed. You have had the support of two Kings of England. This ship, and the other two anchored nearby, have been lent to you by rich and powerful men. They all believe in your dream."

Mr Phips sighed. "My dream has ended, Francis. This is my second expedition. We have searched the area for three weeks and found nothing. No sign of the pinnacle of rock. Not a single silver coin. As their captain, you must tell the men, Francis."

"Tell them what?"

"I want you to tell them that we are going home tomorrow."

"But why?"

"We will never find the *Concepcion*. It was a silly notion. I will die a poor man."

There were tears in the older man's eyes. Francis couldn't keep his secret any longer. A smile broke over his face.

"I would never have thought of you as

a cruel man, Francis," said Phips. "Why do you laugh at my misery?"

Francis pulled a heavy rectangular shape from under his coat. He put it on the table and slid it across towards Mr Phips. The older man's eyes widened in disbelief. There in front of him was a shining bar of silver.

"One of the divers brought it up today," said Francis. "I believe we have found your treasure, Mr Phips!"  end

During the 16th and 17th centuries, Spain plundered over 16 million kg of silver from Mexico.

THE *CONCEPCION* was a Spanish galleon that left Veracruz in 1641 laden with silver from Mexican silver mines. The ship was wrecked on a reef called Los Abrojos during a hurricane.

William Phips was once a ship's carpenter who couldn't read. He started searching for the wreck 45 years after the *Concepcion* sank. By that time, the wreck and the "pinnacle of rock" that marked it, had been covered with coral. This made it difficult to find.

When Phips finally did locate it, divers brought up ingots of silver and chests and bags full of coins from the wreck. In all they found more than 3000 kg of silver as well as gold and jewels (worth about $2 million today).

Phips knew there was more treasure trapped in the ship's hull, but he couldn't reach it. He tried to devise a way to explode gunpowder underwater, but failed. Phips had to be content with a knighthood and a tenth share of the treasure he'd already found (the rest went to the king). The reef where the *Concepcion* sank became known as the Silver Shoals.

At the bottom of the sea

Many thousands of ships have
sunk with valuable cargoes, and
tonnes of treasure has ended up
at the bottom of the sea. Spanish
galleons laden with gold and
silver sank regularly around
America. Whole fleets came to
grief in the hurricanes of the
Caribbean.

Over the centuries, people have tried to
find the sunken treasure. In earlier times,
treasure hunters were limited because
they didn't have diving equipment.
Nowadays, scuba diving equipment is
readily available and there are mini-
submarines that can take treasure hunters
to depths of several kilometres.

Treasure hunters

Finding sunken treasure can become an
obsession. Instead of simply looking for
adventure many underwater searchers
hope to make vast fortunes. Some
historians feel that treasure hunters
are little better than pirates. They
may damage or destroy artefacts in
their rush to get to any bounty.

> **artefact:**
>
> *an object or tool
> of archaeological
> interest.*

Much treasure is up for sale. You can buy pieces-of-eight and doubloons on the Internet. A piece-of-eight costs between US$150–550 depending on how well the coin was made and if it shows signs of wear.

Pieces-of-eight and doubloons

When buried or sunken treasure is mentioned in stories and films, it is often described as pieces-of-eight or Spanish doubloons. What exactly are they?

The unit of Spanish currency in the 16th and 17th centuries was the *reale*. The silver coins transported on the treasure ships were each worth eight reales and so became known as pieces-of-eight.

Gold coins were measured in *escudos*, where one escudo equalled 10 reales. The term doubloon came from the Spanish word for "double" as each coin was worth double the value of the coin below it.

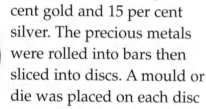

Doubloons were made up of 85 per cent gold and 15 per cent silver. The precious metals were rolled into bars then sliced into discs. A mould or die was placed on each disc

and then struck with a heavy hammer to
impress the image into the metal. The
manufacturers were mostly concerned
that the weight of the precious metal in
the coin was accurate. Whether the coin
was circular or the design centred was
not important, and no two are the same.

Silver Shoals

The bulk of the *Concepcion* treasure was
found by an American named Burt D.
Webber Jr, 300 years after William Phips's
time. Webber was well-prepared and
made use of modern technology. Before
he started diving, Webber spent a number
of years searching Spanish records. He
also read the newly discovered journal
from Francis Rogers's ship, the *Henry*. He
used a device called a **magnetometer**
which detects metal objects.

Just like William Phips, Burt Webber
took two expeditions to find the wreck. In
his first expedition, he found thirteen
other ships—but no sign of the
Concepcion. On his second
expedition, Webber was luckier.
Within the first week he found
the wreck of the *Concepcion*.

magnetometer:
*an instrument using
magnetic fields to
detect metal objects.*

Using modern equipment, he had no trouble getting to the treasure in the hold. Over a period of eleven months, he salvaged thousands of silver coins and a thousand pieces of jewellery. His expeditions cost him US$450,000, but he found treasure worth nearly US$14 million.

Tobermory galleon

In 1588, the Spanish sent a big fleet of ships to fight against the English. The English had fewer ships but still managed to soundly defeat the Spanish. The English ships then blocked the English Channel. The Spanish ships were forced to sail around Scotland and Ireland to get back to Spain. Though only three ships were sunk in the battle, 23 were lost on the voyage home because of terrible storms.

One galleon took shelter in Tobermory Bay, off the Scottish Isle of Mull. A local Scottish clan agreed to help the Spanish sailors fix the ship. Repairs were going well when the ship suddenly exploded. Legend says that a Scottish chieftain's wife blew the ship up because her husband had fallen in love with a Spanish princess on the ship.

> The Spanish Armada was a large fleet of armed ships sent by Spain to invade England in 1588. The Armada was defeated.

One hundred and fifty years later, in 1729, though no-one could remember the ship's name, the fact that it was a treasure ship hadn't been forgotten. A man called Jacob Rowe became interested in the Tobermory galleon. He invented a "diving engine" so that he could search for sunken treasure. His "diving engine" was a copper tube with leather sleeves. The diver was locked inside and lowered to the seabed. Jacob Rowe didn't find any treasure.

Another 200 years passed before a team of treasure hunters found the Tobermory wreck again and excavated it. They didn't find any treasure either.

Searching the library for treasure

Instead of searching the seabed, these adventurers would have been better off searching the libraries. Detailed records of the Spanish Armada can be found in Spanish archives. If the treasure hunters had searched the

> **archive:**
> a collection of official records stored in a safe place.

archives, they would have found that the *San Juan de Sicilia* carried no treasure. Research would have told them they were wasting their time and it would have saved them a lot of money as well.

Pirate wreck

Remember the pirate Samuel Bellamy? He ended up at the bottom of the sea with his stolen ship the *Whydah*. He didn't get to rest in peace though. Like many treasure ships, the *Whydah* attracted treasure hunters.

In many parts of the world, shipwrecks are protected by law.

The wreck was found buried under metres of sand in 1984 by the professional treasure hunter, Barry Clifford. Thousands of coins were recovered from the wreck as well as much gold jewellery.

Some historians believe that the most important finds on the wreck were not the treasure, but the everyday items which tell us something about life as a pirate. Among the items found on the *Whydah* were elegant pistols, a leather pouch, a silk stocking and a teapot.

All that glitters

Not all treasure is made of gold, silver and precious stones.

A Vietnamese fisherman accidentally came across the wreck of a Chinese junk in the 1980s. He was fishing near Vung Tau in South Vietnam when he found porcelain bowls buried in lumps of concretion. He carefully chipped away the sand and shells and sold the bowls to an antique dealer. He then went back to search for more.

A bell and other items from a shipwreck concreted with sand and shells after many years on the seabed.

When the Vietnamese Government heard about an unusual amount of antique Chinese porcelain being offered for sale, they sent someone to investigate. There were still thousands of pieces of chinaware at the wreck site, most of it still intact.

Historians believe that the ship was sunk around 1690 while transporting the porcelain from China to Europe. The cargo included thousands of blue and white tea bowls, pill boxes, teapots, soup spoons and small figures. The salvaged chinaware was auctioned in 1992 for over US$7 million.

junk:

a type of ship used in China.

concretion:

sand and stones pressed together into a hard layer, like concrete.

Modern treasure

Sunken treasure isn't all from ships that sank centuries ago. Plenty of modern ships have gone to the bottom of the ocean with cargoes of gold and diamonds on board.

The British Royal Mail Steam Packet Company's ship the *Douro* was returning to England in 1883 after a trip to South America. There were only 55 passengers on board, but the ship was also carrying a load of gold sovereigns, gold bars and £25,000 worth of diamonds.

It was a clear night with a full moon but somehow the chief officer didn't see a Spanish ship ploughing towards them. The two ships collided and a huge hole was ripped in the side of the *Douro*. The collision forced the Spanish ship back, but her engines were still running so she crashed into the *Douro* again. Within ten minutes, the *Douro* was sinking stern first. Thirty-six passengers and crew were lost.

Grabbing gold

No-one tried to locate the *Douro* until 1979 when Englishman Nigel Pickford decided to try and salvage the ship's treasure. He spent years looking through newspapers, logbooks and shipping registers for clues.

He began searching the seabed with sonar equipment, scanners and submarine cameras in 1993. Once he found the *Douro* he used a camera-guided grab to go down to the seabed and in through the hole in the side of the ship. The first grab came up with some plates and wine bottles, but no gold. On the second attempt, the machine's jaws came back full of gold. Pickford recovered all the gold bars and most of the sovereigns. There was no trace of the diamonds, which are still at the bottom of the ocean somewhere.

> The word sonar stands for <u>SO</u>und <u>N</u>avigation <u>A</u>nd <u>R</u>anging. It is used to detect things underwater by sending out sound waves which bounce back off any solid objects.

Andrea Doria again

Remember the ocean liner, the *Andrea Doria*, that also sunk after a collision? There were rumours that the ship's vaults were full of jewels and money. In 1985, a team of hunters braved the deep water to excavate the ship.

The team found the ship's safe, and it was full of money.

> A grab is a device with hinged metal jaws for gripping objects. It is lowered to the seabed but operated from on board a ship.

Unfortunately, it was very soggy paper money, which no longer had any value.

Another shipwreck rumoured to be full of gold was the Dutch liner *Tubantic*, sunk by a German torpedo during the First World War. Though the ship's records stated that the *Tubantic* was carrying a cargo of cheeses, salvagers were convinced that £2 million worth of gold and diamonds were being smuggled inside the cheeses. They spent ten years searching the wreck, but all they found was wet cheese!

Finders keepers

It would be wonderful to find tonnes of gold and silver and become very rich. This is what has driven treasure hunters for centuries. They work very hard, risk their lives and spend lots of money searching for treasure. Are they entitled to keep their riches? Or is it better to keep

all the finds from a shipwreck together in a museum where everyone can see them? What would you do if you knew where there was sunken treasure?

chapter 6
Shipwreck science

Imagine you are Elias Stadiatis, a Greek sponge diver in the Mediterranean Sea. It is 1900...

Elias put on the stiff canvas diving suit and waited while Captain Kondos fitted the heavy copper helmet in place. It was hot and stuffy in the suit and the air that came to him in the narrow tube smelt of oil and rubber. Sometimes the air tube wrapped around pieces of coral and the air supply was cut off. That was very scary, but most of the time Elias liked diving. His father and his grandfather had both been sponge divers, but they didn't have diving suits in their day. They just had to hold their breath.

The best divers could hold their breath for up to five minutes.

Captain Kondos tapped on the face glass of the helmet and gave Elias the thumbs up. Elias lowered himself slowly into the water. Once he was in the water he didn't mind the discomfort of the heavy suit or the stale air. He just loved being underwater.

Elias had never dived in this spot before. Captain Kondos had chosen this new place to dive, just north of the tiny island of Antikythera, because the sponges had run out at their regular diving place. The water was clear and blue. Elias enjoyed looking at the beautiful coral and the striped fish as he descended to the seabed. He landed on the bottom with a jolt. Now it was time to go to work.

He looked around for the sponges. It was hard to imagine that such shapeless, motionless things were actually living sea creatures. He picked up three or four sponges and put them in his collection bag. Then he saw something that made him gasp with horror. There, on the seabed in front of him, was an arm, pale and bloodless. He looked around. There was the naked body of a woman with her legs missing, and a horse's head. He realised that he was surrounded by gruesome body parts. What terrible place had he discovered? Some dumping ground for murdered people? He tried to get away from the awful place, but he couldn't swim in the heavy suit. He yanked the air line three times. He waited. He yanked the air line again. Finally he felt himself being hauled up. He moved up in slow motion towards the surface above him. It seemed to take forever to get back up to the boat.

Finally four strong arms pulled him up onto the deck of the boat and anxious fingers undid the helmet. Elias threw off the helmet.

"Dead people and horses!" he cried. "Naked women. Many bodies."

Captain Kondos and the other divers looked at him perplexed.

"Go and see for yourself," said Elias. "I'm not going down there ever again."

None of the divers would go down. Captain Kondos had to climb into the diving suit and descend himself. He took the end of a length of rope down with him. A few minutes later, Elias felt a tug on the rope. He hauled it up, dreading what terrible thing he might find tied to the end. The other men helped and together they pulled the object in like a fish. They gathered around. Lying on the deck was a human arm—not one of flesh and bone, but one made from bronze.

end

T HE SPONGE DIVER HAD found the wreck of an ancient Roman trading ship. Though very little of the boat remained, much of the ship's cargo was still intact. The ship had been full of bronze and marble statues. With such an old ship, there are no records to tell us about its voyage. Archaeologists estimate that it is from the first century A.D.—nearly 2000 years old.

Elias was a real person. He was a poor sponge diver, but his name will always be remembered among divers and historians as the man who found the Antikythera wreck.

Mystery gadget

As well as the statues, the sponge divers also found a remarkable device. They think it is a complex astronomical calculator which predicts the movement of stars and planets. Historians were very surprised to find that people so long ago had the knowledge to make such an intricate scientific instrument. As no-one knows exactly what it is, it is known as the "Antikythera mechanism". The statues and the mechanism are on display in the National Museum in Athens.

Marine archaeology

Imagine how surprised people from the first century would have been if they had known that almost 2000 years later people would find their lost cargo and bring it up from the ocean bed.

The Antikythera wreck made historians think carefully about shipwrecks. After finding such old and interesting things on the bottom of the sea, they began to realise that shipwrecks held all kinds of historical items. As other ancient shipwrecks were found, archaeologists became interested and the study of marine archaeology began.

Underwater time capsules

One problem with archaeology sites on land is that they are often burial places or rubbish tips. They don't usually contain items from people's everyday life. There are a few exceptions such as Pompeii, where the lava from an erupting volcano

marine archaeology:
studying the past by examining sunken ships and their contents.

caught the inhabitants going about their daily lives. Pompeii is like a time capsule.

At the bottom of the sea there are thousands of shipwrecks. These can also be time capsules. If the ship is well-preserved, divers can find cabins and cargoes just as they were when the ship sank. Even if most of the ship has disintegrated, some items still remain. Historians can get clues about nautical instruments, personal possessions and cargoes at the time of the shipwreck.

> The pressure of the sea on the *Titanic* is 4000 tonnes per square metre. If you were standing on the wreck the weight of the water would be like having 10 elephants on your head.

As the British underwater archaeologist Peter Throckmorton said, "It has become the destiny of the ships that did not arrive to tell the story of those that did."

Digging in the deep

Treasure hunters blast and dredge shipwrecks. Marine archaeologists look more carefully through the wreckage. They realise that a wealth of historical artefacts lie at the bottom of the sea. The first shipwreck to be scientifically investigated was a

Wreckage lying on the sea floor.

The Bronze Age, (4500 B.C–500 B.C.) was when tools and weapons were made from bronze. The Bronze Age ended when iron became the commonly used metal.

Bronze Age ship in waters off Cape Gelidonya in Turkey in 1958. Scientists carefully mapped and photographed the shipwreck site and recorded the location of every item before it was removed.

History on the seabed

When the *Thetis* was wrecked on 26 May 1848, two children were washed away in the darkness and drowned. This child's shoe was recovered from the wreck.

Marine archaeologists want to learn the whole story of a wreck: how the ship was built, what its cargo was, how the sailors on board lived. To them, the value of a pirate's stocking or a rusted astrolabe is greater than any gold coin, because they can learn something about the past.

All sorts of items have survived in shipwrecks. On the *Mary Rose* archaeologists found leather shoes, pewter flagons, a miniature sundial, musical instruments, the oldest known ship's compass and a backgammon set. On the Bronze Age Cape Gelidonya wreck, copper ingots, Egyptian scarabs, a razor and olive pips were found.

Which is the oldest wreck?

The oldest known shipwreck is 3400 years old. This ship was sailing when Tutankhamen was alive. It was found near the Turkish Cape of Uluburun in 1984 by Dr George Bass. Dr Bass has found and carefully investigated many ancient shipwrecks. He has been described as an "underwater Indiana Jones". Some of the things archaeologists found were: swords, jewellery, pottery, blue and purple glass and a golden goblet.

Modern salvage techniques

It wasn't until 1985 that the *Titanic*, the best known shipwreck of all, could be investigated. A piloted, submersible vessel called *Alvin*, was used to reach the *Titanic* which is more than four kilometres beneath the surface. It took *Alvin* two hours to descend to that depth. Remotely operated vehicles (ROVs) with spotlights were sent out from *Alvin* to video the ship which

Remotely Operated Vehicles (ROVs) are unmanned machines used to salvage items from the seabed. They are used in waters where it is too deep to dive. ROVs can go down to a depth of 6000 metres.

had been at the bottom of the ocean since 1912. Millions of people around the world watched the eerie voyage around the sunken liner on television. Perhaps you have seen some of this film footage in documentaries about the *Titanic*. Diamonds worth US$5 million went down with the *Titanic*. No doubt salvagers are planning how to find them. Some people think that shipwrecks like the *Titanic*, where many people died, should be treated as cemeteries and left undisturbed.

Conservation

Items that have been in seawater for many years, sometimes centuries, can disintegrate when they are brought up into the air. They have to be treated immediately if they are to survive. Lead shot from the *Mary Rose* became hot, fizzed and started to fall apart when taken out of the sea. Glass beads from a Phoenician wreck which had been in the sea for nearly 3000 years, exploded into particles of dust when they were dried out. Once removed from the sea, wood will shrink, crack and warp. Each item removed from a shipwreck must be chemically treated to conserve it. Different substances need different treatment.

It was once believed that wood could only survive for a few years underwater, that after 50 years it would all be eaten by shipworm. It is now known that if the wreck is protected by a layer of sand or mud, wood can last for centuries.

Raised from the dead

The Swedish warship *Vasa*, launched in 1628, was a work of art, covered with 700 carvings. As a sailing vessel it was a complete failure. On its maiden voyage it stayed afloat for 1.5 km and then sank. It had been poorly designed and was top-heavy.

Nearly 300 years later, in 1961, spectators watched in amazement as the almost complete hull of the *Vasa* was raised from the waters of the Baltic Sea.

The remains of the ship were kept in an air-conditioned building on land. It was sprayed with 20,000 litres of chilled water every minute so that

> The *Vasa* is the biggest wooden artefact that has ever been raised from the seabed.

Tiny bacteria are eating away at the *Titanic*. Every day they devour about 0.1 of a tonne of iron from the wreck. In about 90 years the 25,000 tonne wreck will collapse.

it didn't dry out and warp. The ship was then carefully treated with a special preserving wax called polyethylene glycol or PEG. To make sure it didn't rot on the inside, the chemical had to penetrate right through the wood. The PEG was sprayed over the entire hull once every day for fifteen years. Only then were those preserving the *Vasa* confident they could safely let the ship dry out.

Can shipwrecks have worms?

Shipworms or teredo worms are small, hungry, wood-boring animals like tiny snails. They eat their way through the wood in ships whether the ship is sailing on the ocean or lying at the bottom of the sea. Shipworms like to live in warm, salty water. They thrive in the Tropics.

Ships used to be coated with a mixture of tar, tallow and sulphur two or three times a year to protect them from shipworm. Another method was to cover the

Davy Jones's locker:

the bottom of the ocean, especially when referring to it as the grave of all who perish at sea.

ship's hull with a thin layer of copper.

When wooden ships sink, these worms keep eating until there is nothing left.

The hull of the *Vasa* survived because the Baltic Sea is very cold and has a low salt content, so shipworms don't live there.

The seabed is a rich source of artefacts that give us clues about what life was like in the past.

Unlocking Davy Jones's locker

Thousands and thousands of ships have sunk over the centuries. The remains of ships from all ages are waiting to be discovered and investigated. There is enough historical material to keep marine archaeologists busy for a very long time. Modern technology lets us discover wrecks that were previously unreachable. It also helps preserve what we find so that we, and future generations, will be able to learn more about our history.

Where to from here?

If you would like to find out more about shipwrecks, a good place to start is your local library. There are some original accounts of shipwrecks in the following books:

Huntress, Keith (ed.). *Narratives of Shipwrecks and Disasters 1586-1860.* Iowa State University Press, 1974.

Neider, Charles (ed.). *Great Shipwrecks and Castaways: Authentic Accounts of Disasters at Sea.* Dorset Press, New York, 1990 (original edition 1952).

Maritime museums contain exhibits about ships and the sea. They often have shipwreck remains or whole ships so that you can imagine what life on board might be like.

Look on the Web too. Some sites list all the wrecks in a particular area. Other sites are about one particular shipwreck. Type 'shipwrecks' in the search box and see what you come up with!

For a good story about shipwrecks, read the companion volume in the Phenomena series *Deepwater*.

Carole's note

While researching this book I learnt about many things besides shipwrecks. I learnt about how ships have been built, how sea battles were fought and how sailors lived on board ship. I also learnt about people and the different ways they react to extreme situations.

Whenever I could, I tried to read the accounts written by the actual people who experienced shipwreck, rather than someone else's idea of what it might have been like.

One of the most exciting moments was the discovery of a copy of William Strachey's account of the wreck of the *Sea Venture* in a library near where I live. It was 375 years old, being printed in 1625, only 16 years after the actual event. I had to read it in a special room in the library and wear gloves to turn the pages. The account really made me feel what it would be like to be on a ship that was about to sink.

Index